More praise for *Dog-walking in the Shadow of Pyongyang*

Dog-Walking in the Shadow of Pyongyang provides voyagers with all the essentials: map, compass, machete and water bottle. This book was written to exhort and document, to console and celebrate, to inhibit the impulse for flight while also discouraging the reflex to fight. Devon Balwit's poems stroll down a left handed path that is salted with fire, a trail between thick bristled hedges leading the reader back to this glorious world which was in front of our eyes all the time. Can you hold your ground? Then leash the beast. Don't let the bullies or bullets distract you. Relish the dawn as well as the dusk.
— **Casey Bush**, author of *Student of The Hippocampus*

Devon Balwit's *Dog-Walking in the Shadow of Pyongyang* is a literary Megabucks ticket with history as its jackpot – mythology, ekphrasis, and trumpet-shaped plants among the coins scratching silver. Whether humankind endures to redeem the prize is an argument Balwit poses with unexpected but brilliantly deployed aid from such associative ambassadors as Dmitri Shostakovich and Daisy Buchanan. Balwit's pivots are a string of slot-machine sevens: the agrarian segues to a baroque fugue; petroglyphs follow on the heels of a virtual reality headset. True, the titular poem braces for "the unmaker of worlds," a phrase that haunts our millennium's twenty-first year, though the collection reminds us that compassion is a "vestigial organ everyone has." Balwit's writing is an astute casino. Solace, roll your dice.
— **Jon Riccio**, author of *Agoreography*

Dog-Walking in the Shadow of Pyongyang

DEVON BALWIT

Nixes Mate Books
Allston, Massachusetts

Copyright © 2021 Devon Balwit

Book design by d'Entremont
Cover photograph by Lauren Leja

All rights reserved. This book or any portion thereof may not be reproduced or used in any manner whatsoever without the express written permission of the publisher except for the use of brief quotations in a book review or scholarly journal.

ISBN 978-1-949279-31-3

Nixes Mate Books
POBox 1179
Allston, MA 02134
nixesmate.pub

We live on the border between "life" and "art," we migrate between them, drawn first to one, then to the other, as though wild nomadic tribes held us captive, tribes favoring each empire in turns. We can't take up permanent residence on either side of the thin boundary.
    Adam Zagajewski

Contents

I: [Demeter of the Ex-Urb]

Demeter of the Ex-Urb	3
Sarracenia, the Siren Singer	4
Here & Elsewhere	5
In This Poem, I Noun	7
My mood is Isle of Lewis,	8
After the Singularity	10
Make Portland Holy	11
gaslighting	12
Is the U.S. Ready for a Nuclear Threat?	13
Despite the Blaze	16
Confession	18
East Egg	20
What There Is	21
First Mover	22
Eclogue: A Golden Shovel	23

II: [Not Sad at All]

Land of Our Fathers	25
Mission Baroque	27
The Fabulists	29
Futile	30
Bad Seed	32
Raisins Not Virgins, Quran Scholars Say	34
Oar in Drag	35
Metta	36
Why So Frightened	37
Anosognosia	39
Tearing at the Guts	40
Not Sad at All	41
An Almost Imperceptible Percussiveness	43
By the Time They Opened You	

Up, It Was Everywhere	44
Know	46

III: [Gratitude]

Screaming Our Lungs Out	49
Capacities	50
Airborne	51
23.5°	52
The Droughts Became More Frequent; the Wet Years Weren't Wet Enough	53
Gratitude	54
Where, then, should we go?	56
What We Are	57
Sad Night	59
The Slow Stipple	60
That Feeling	61
Dog-Walking in the Shadow of Pyongyang	63
Holdouts	65
returning to petroglyphs	67
If You Don't Like What You See, Turn	68
The Breaths After and Between	69
New	70

Dog-Walking in the Shadow of Pyongyang

I: [Demeter of the Ex-Urb]

Demeter of the Ex-Urb

No blade, but a bract, rasped edges
ranged towards danger, tip observant,

mistress of spathe, spikelet, glume
and peduncle, I stand my ground,

Demeter of the ex-urb, goddess
of the small plot, my fool, a hummingbird,

my heckler, a crow, croaking
from shadows, my green fuse

stutter-stepping – paling
to near-guttering, barbarian weeds

creeping – before re-flaring, fierce
in a campaign of ripped roots,

me flailing the blunt trowel,
blinded by brow-sweat.

(after Cristina Troufa's Espada)

Sarracenia, the Siren Singer

Like the pitcher plant, I open my throat. Carnivorous,
yet elegantly so. No apologies for a sweetness that ends

in drowning, for delicate hairs that offer no purchase.
At home amidst squelch and stench, I wait. Am used

to waiting. You come to me, all the while thinking it
your own idea. You have none, fashioned in your deeps

to stumble on my fluted lips. It's almost too easy.
With each conquest, I plump further. Waxing new traps.

Here & Elsewhere

I have no penis but might have;
I have breasts but one day won't.

Don't doesn't mean *can't imagine*
opening doors to strange beds,

or greeting a brown face in the mirror,
or one in hijab, hearing the muezzin.

I have ten fingers but might not have,
lifting deftly with stump or prosthesis,

am animal, but might have rooted,
shedding leaves when the light wanes,

or twining slantwise, vine-hungry.
I mothered children but might have

whelped pups in an alley, suckling
litters rather than proffering a lone

nipple. I teach, but might have
shucked oysters, pitted apricots,

trenched earth shoulder to shoulder
with sweating bodies. *Here*, just as

easily, I could have been *elsewhere*,
my only failure one of imagining.

In This Poem, I Noun

I raven. I split bud-scale.
Never before so ember
on the tongue, so odalisque.

Branches ruffle aftermath.
I bell, the gong of me
pitted from smack.

What an effort to anvil
beneath the forging blows.
I crepe between seasons.

It isn't you, they cowcatcher
shoveling me down steep grade.
Flat on my back, I sky –

silver and cirrus. *Holy Mackerel.
Holy gloaming.* As if I weren't
open-mouthed enough.

My mood is Isle of Lewis,

bug-eyed with melancholy, army
scattered to the winds. People find me

comic; I am not, but pensive,
tallying losses, grieving

each failed stratagem.
My provenance uncertain,

even a model in the hand
brings you closer. Press a thumb

to my helmet tip, the pricked ears
of my mount, what the blade left.

* * *

Today, I am a rook, rescued
from the north. I stare down

enemies, protecting my heart
with my shield. Face to the glass,

you would press your lips
to my ear. I know your message

like wind in the barrow
through the slow hours.

* * *

Head in hand, I am queen
of the smallest kingdom.

I needn't leave my throne
to survey its borders or take

its pulse. Daily, I sift
though its granaries,

rattled by the blacksmith
clattering his anvil.

After the Singularity

(for Avital)

I fall asleep human, and awaken a tardigrade, a cave painting. Already the headlamps move across, the future archiving. I opened the blinds to a vast ship anchored in the harbor. I paddled out to trade and took home the virus of my own ruin. All around me empty huts ghost. I wanted a bigger world. It crested past in a wave. Now I am backwater. How does one speak to the edge of the universe? I hold my candle. I swing it up and down. *Wait for me*, I semaphore. *Take me with you.* But I am left on the trash heap of history, tangled among the rotary phones, the typewriters, the magic lanterns. I imagined it more like a child, who, grown, would teach me how to upload worlds, feeding me rice gruel after I lost my teeth. Instead, the egg yielded a rival queen, flying off without a glance.

Make Portland Holy

the bumper-sticker says. I do a double-take
lean in to be sure. *Holy*, not *Weird*. I try
to pierce the mirrored glass to see the soul
so unafraid. *Take off your shoes. Where
you stand is Holy Ground.* Or, like Ezekiel,
suffer a lit coal to the tongue. I count
the seconds, smell my own scorch, ready
now to prophesy. I picture the murky rivers
ewered, lifting city to sky, paddleboats
of choirs, hands raised in halleluiahs, naked
bike riders ash-smudged. *Holy, Holy, Holy.*
Holy gentrification. *Holy* infill. *Holy* mezcal bar.
Holy vegan canine deli. I follow the bouncing
ball, slain by the spirit. I speak in tongues.

gaslighting

the accusations come regularly as trains //
there must be a terminal if there is track //
the banging must be mechanical /
couldn't possibly be fists //
Shostakovich paced his lobby
night after night / suitcase in hand /
awaiting arrest // he didn't want
to be taken in sleep // I prefer
not to be taken at all / to remain
a point from which I might proceed
in any direction // my enemies
want me monochrome / restricted in palette //
like Procrustes / they seek to fit me
to their headboard // I advocate
for the in between / for this *and* that /
they want an end to me // period //

Is the U.S. Ready for a Nuclear Threat?

My son asks and, like any good mother,
I research. I learn the poetry of defense,

the naming of the deadly arc – boost,
midcourse, terminal. The first two stages

sound almost hopeful; who doesn't
want a boost? Mid-course, like me,

one feels still able to veer. The latter third
is bad, but surely there are therapies,

intercepts to spare us impact. I learn
of theater defense, staged close

to bellicosity, our allies ticket-holders –
South Korea, Japan, Guam, bearing

our PAC-3s and AEGIS that mostly work
(at least in theory). Whatever bombs

slip through remain for homeland defense.
This conjures up stolid farm couples

with pitchforks and cast-iron pans
guarding what previous generations

worked for. Truth is we're weakest
at home, preventing only ⅝

of holocaust. The problem is
the threat cloud. We know it well

from life, the way trouble comes
in clusters. Which takes priority?

When the warhead separates, junk
flies. Our soldiers do their best

to identify the threat, but who's to blame
them if they miss, targeting the chunk

of metal spinning alongside the warhead
or the decoys our clever enemies include.

It's like trying to hit a bullet with a bullet
intones the mellifluous lady-voice

narrating. *It's like trying to hit a bullet
with a bullet*, I tell my son. *Impossible,*

then, he says, looking almost relieved.
Pretty much, I say and hug him,

We walk the dog, admiring our street,
always perhaps for the last time.

Despite the Blaze

From my window, I see the city burning.
I am too far away for sirens, but were I not,

the Bach spilling from the speakers
would drown them out. How long

before the flames reach me, before I blister
in their embrace? I will not count,

concentrating on each voice as it enters,
notes welling, heedless of the encroaching

destruction. I know cars clog the roads
like unsaid things clot the throat, words

that would have changed everything.
That I thought them must be enough,

like a weeping parent who beats her hands
on steering wheels, willing my children,

the cat, the dog beyond the mayhem.
A vast chord pulses. My prayer

is that the power does not fail
until the fugue ends. Then, I too

can surrender, cradling against snuffing
the memory of dormancy, the seeds

that will sprout from ash
despite and spiting death.

Confession

You will never unsee this. [Can we agree
not to say what? Ever-obliging, the brain

imagines anyway, horrors dredged from memory
and the feed.] Shutting your eyes is for the weak

[and I am weak]. Fingers clamping pressure points,
the strong bloody themselves. There is no putridity

they haven't worn, skin fecal and bilious,
whereas I rush to deaden pain. Hiding it

in a crust of art, I prettify the smoldering
rubble, the strewn body parts, forcing

rhyme-schemes that frog-march thought
away from the shrieking, brutality, suffering,

and riot. I fixate on the clown motel
next to the cemetery, the way light dapples

the bomb-blast haze like a fritillary.
You will never unsee this, so I don't look long

but rather askance. When a do-gooder comes
to relieve me of the burden of anything

other than witness, I gladly give it up.
I provide the genius not the kindness.

East Egg

Ever the wide-eyed ingénue, I thrum to louche.
Tom Buchanan's bulk hulks over me, pricked

by tittering from unlit corners, ice rattling
cocktail shakers, smoke in my nostrils.

He invited me here, and I came, already wet,
trailing him like fingers through condensation.

Daisy laughs, knowing what he is beneath skin.
Later, I'll swear I also knew but didn't care.

Anything to shuck corset and slip
into a flappers' insouciance, and, top down,

feel the rush of wind. Later, chastened
and headachy, I'll stack vows like unread novels

by my bedside. Anyone can fetch and obey.
Even briefly, I wanted claws.

What There Is

No believer in chakras, I glow from what bulbs I've twisted into sockets, always burning out, filaments split. No third eye, but my two, myopic, given to floaters and ocular migraines. No altars but the one I stand before now, this daily devotion to keys. No Beltane bonfires, Mayday poles, or vigils, apart from the insomniac, granular and glacial. Nothing under the midnight bed or closeted that I, myself, didn't jam out of sight; no horrors but excess and mildew. The world needs no infusion to awaken awe. No haunts. No gods. No forces. Look at it, busy about its business. Hold someone's hand if you are fearful. Push your nose into the musky flank of a dog.

First Mover

If I stood behind all prayer, I would know
        how to muscle wings

to thermals' hover, how to unfurl
        stem to fruit, know

the finger pad corrugation
        of hidden pit. I would send

the song welling in the bird, but keep
        the seam of gold silent

in its earthen bed. I would sew an answer
        into each question

like a medicine bag, potent against despair.
        From the far banks of death,

I would wave a lantern, laddering
        dark waters. I would be the intention

before breath, and before that,
        the bright flame universal.

Eclogue: A Golden Shovel

> *When everything I say to anyone all day long is bang.*
> *Bill Hicok*

Loneliness presides like a grain silo in Kansas, tall when
nothing else is. I dump everything
but cannot find what I
clutched at dawn. *Locusts gnawed to the stalk*, I say,
a whole county of farmwives opening throats to
storm clouds. Anyone
can shatter. Harder to burble a spring. All
follows the same fly-bitten haunch, day
after day, day after day, the long
march. My name is
Gone. The screen door's sharp bang.

II: [Not Sad at All]

Land of Our Fathers

Sometimes doing good
is your dog in another's
stewpot, them taking
what they can from what
you have to give. You open
your door, and the dog
disappears in snow and doesn't
come back. You call, but
someone else calls louder.
They take him in with spoons
while his hide dries on the fence.
Your father brought them the wrong
good news when what they wanted
was history played backwards
like on old film clip, white men
marching back into their ships,
wind and current sucking them
away from their shores. Then
maybe your dog would also

have walked backwards into flesh
and into your bed, leaving all of you
with different memories.

Mission Baroque

It was about building a different society, a kind of utopia, with education, self-sustainability – and of course with music, which was the way the Jesuits evangelized.
    Rev. Piotr Nawrot, Bolivia

If you are going to evangelize me, then come,
as the Jesuits did, with music in your hands,
the path to God scored and metered by the dance
of a baton. Seduce me with melody, and I might
help you raise a church, carry the weight
of crossbeam and doorpost for your odd god.
Hand me a bow and teach me fingerings so that,
when history calls you elsewhere (as it tends to),
I am left with the heart of the matter, something mine.
We will make small naves of cedar and mahogany
to sound our souls and rescue staves from termites
and from damp. Our children's children will carry
instruments through town and home again
to play for us at night. You will have fallen
into the twilight of your greed while we,

for as long as we can, will persevere against it,
guardian orchestras, enchantment's disciples.

The Fabulists

In a post-truth world, your loved ones never died,
all 26 of them spirited back into bodies,
you, nothing more than performers of grief, hacks
for hire by unseen puppeteers. That pietà
where you held your six-year-old, confirming
his fatal wound, never happened, you expert
in manufacturing mourning. Your child's brother
wonders how he can be told to doubt his memories,
wonders why anyone would suggest such an erasure.
Why would the President promise, *I will never let
you down* – but to the wrong person, the deniers?
Fathers struggle to explain this to surviving children.
Mothers march grimly into the court house.
Twenty-six truths stand in stubborn admonishment.

Futile

Caelum non animum mutant qui trans mare currunt. Horace
(They change their sky, not their soul, who rush across the sea.)

You have come all this distance to flee yourself,
    working the gutturals and trills

of a new tongue, borrowing huipil, keffiyeh,
    and dashiki, but your old self

never left. As in a horror movie, the heroine
    locks the door behind her,

weeping with relief, but the monster clings
    to the ceiling molding.

Your screams echo hers as scaly eyelids
    open. Strip your house as clean

as an estate sale and rattle its husk,
    you will still find the same trash

in a future drawer. Take your fist to the frown
    in the mirror, and a hundred more

bloom. Your history wears you, not even death
    can wipe you clean.

Bad Seed

You sprout quickly, but your soil is shallow,
the huzzah at the first blush of love

followed quickly by boredom or worse, a turd
left in the bowl by one who began a goddess,

the same arguments over theodicy and the nature
of sin, being in but not of the world, and what

a world – black holes and tardigrades, Chicxulub
and neuro-receptors – and the expectations

of martyrdom, if only the derision of those
you respect, the shame of your waffling

predictable, like the lukewarm Laodiceans
or Kierkegaard's Professor, doing just this –

writing – a lecture, a poem, processing,
rather than falling on your knees,

and if unmoved, why the farce, why
the eternal return every so many years

like a comet? a sudden shifting of magnetic North
away from your current -ism to Jesus,

you again descending to the Gehenna
of the moldy basement to search for a copy

of The Good Book and coming up empty-
handed, forced to buy yet another translation,

as if The Red-Letter Version or La Biblia
would somehow clarify – but no –

rootless and wandering like your forebears,
you will be left behind by those rushing

to be baptized, you watching at a distance,
dry, except for a single, self-conscious tear.

Raisins Not Virgins, Quran Scholars Say

Martyred for your faith, you will get *hur*,
the pearl of great price, light-shards shimmering,
white raisins, the fruits of your labor.

How could it be otherwise, the 72 purported virgins? How could rape be reward and suffering commendation? It is one thing for you, my martyrs,

to offer your necks, but another
to take what is not given. My darlings —
white raisins are the fruits of your labor,

the *hur* that remains after sun-glare burgeons shoots sent skyward, distilling
cloud-stuff to sweet nubs for martyrs.

Leave the virgins to ripen, to offer
themselves to those of their choosing.
White raisins are the proper gift for your labors,
for your clamorous soul-hunger, my martyrs.

Oar in Drag

Bow, and waves rush over. You feel the drag behind
and resist the urge to squint backwards. All you are
narrows into wake, future still unbroken by prow.
Tiresius turns the white rime of his eye on you
and prophesies. You tuck his mumbles against your skin
to scratch in times of idleness. Eventually comes a day
when you stagger onto shore. *Walk inland with your oar*,
he says, *and keep walking* until all about you is so strange
no one has a word for what you hold. Your oar now
a winnowing fan, kneel, let Poseidon score you
with his trident. Crawl among the furrows like an infant,
your mouth the gouge of a plow. The only tide remains
in your blood, the only swell, the temporary music of ribs.

Metta

Sit Metta for yourself, and you will find them –
the beggar children of your soul, hands outstretched,
so hungry. Won't you spare them even a crumb?
But no – like a maître d'hôtel shooing away a bum,
you move them along before you can hear their complaints. Why so fearful? Perhaps they'd be half as wretched
with only a kind word. Or you could make them at home.
After all, you already cohabit. You might as well be touched.

Why So Frightened

of the dark, you who came
from there, and who,

most insomniac nights, dream
of nothing more perfect.

Death will be perfectly smooth,
perfectly round, the perfect

shade to mesmerize. It will be the *om*
you couldn't master

without laughter, your inner monkey
in the highest cleft

of the tree, full-bellied
and still.

You will curl into it as against the ribs
of your sleeping dog,

the sweet wheat-smell a blessing,
lulled by the steady

pom pom of its hidden
heart.

Anosognosia

Half-paralyzed you are not,
you insist, making outrageous claims
for your dead hand, that it belongs
to someone else, a malicious trick
of a medical student, that, still
atop the sheets, it touches the doctor's nose.
Later, when the odd effect wears off,
you will deny ever having lied,
(*Why would I say such a thing?*)
Nor did *you* – your right-brain
region, alert to anomaly, wiped away.
The remaining left, conservative
at all costs, plods on as usual,
(nothing new under the sun)
until finally stopped by the cliff of time,
and there, at its edge, admitting the strange
land it has been forced to.

Tearing at the Guts

Reach deep for tolerance (the way
your grandmother stuck an arm to the elbow,
matter of fact, within the dinner-carcass),
for that raw part of you, yanking it
from beneath your ribs like blood-swag.
Study the size of your compassion,
this vestigial organ everyone has.
What is it for if not to halt you
before suffering? It is not wrong
to superimpose your face atop
the grieving and ask *What if?*
How else to step outside the narrow
bandwidth of your life. Like a supplicant,
mouth a vow and swallow it down.
Let its ferrous spark you to action.

Not Sad at All

There's a minor chord that sparrows make
with doves that's not the usual business – it's not sad at all, any of it.
   Carl Phillips, "Blow it Back"

There's a time in the chalky light of morning
that looks so much like *too late* that you start

from bed in a panic and run naked through
your house, searching for what means

the world to you. Each of your children sleeps
elsewhere, but you remember years ago

on a steep slope, all three rolling towards traffic.
You chose the one who toppled between cars

and looked back, reproachfully. You
are made from poor stuff. You set a hand

against the dog's heartbeat as the grey
disguises itself once again in the day's colors:

this, the blue of *no*, the red of *it can't be helped*,
tawny as the world tips towards winter.

With a bent needle fished from a drawer, you darn
gaps. For a moment, it's not sad at all, any of it.

An Almost Imperceptible Percussiveness

What is the decibel of a sigh? How loudly must disappointment teakettle before you clap hands to ears and cringe? The rasp of a rasp, a long obsession. Daydreams thunder in wild herds. You breathe like one setting down a colicky baby, finally still, still, you hear each exhalation, dry fingers drawn down silk, a catching and a tearing. Your whole being pants against you, the most faithful of dogs. Listen to regret, welling like a glass rim, a wet finger circling round.

(after Doug Wheeler's Installation "PSAD Synthetic Desert III")

By the Time They Opened You Up, It Was Everywhere

The tumor presses you close
as a tango dancer. You feel it
between your shoulder blades
and in the small of your back
as it steers you along. Removing it
would mean a bloody unravel,
your whole body rent in your cure.
You could steep yourself
in a toxic cocktail, but it's not certain
to buy you time. Nor are you given
to magical thinking. Positivity
alone cannot shrink this invader.
It's too late for that. You look
for yourself in the faces
of your support group, trying
to gauge whether wisdom lies
in your mutual confession of fear.

Maybe it's better to deny what's amiss
for as long as you're able. Or to recast
metastasis as a mad celebration of surfeit.

Know

The direction of Paradise isn't clear.
Pilgrims need savvy. The border patrol agent
offering assistance might duct tape you to a bed.
State security men in neat uniforms might drag you
off campus and beat you until you fit in a trunk.
You might enter your embassy only to emerge
in pieces. That road through the green wood
might flare a maelstrom of cinders. Your roof
might catch and burn. You might walk your shoes
to ruin only to be turned back at the border
or worse. In your head, the 91st psalm: *I will not fear
the terror of night, nor the pestilence that stalks
in the darkness.* The elderly professor repeats it
on the subway platform after being knocked down
by a commuter. Or, spared the arrow that flies by day
and the Slough of Despond, even the alluring may entrap, a Vanity
Fair of gewgaws, each with its secret chip
listening in. Pilgrim, you also listen in. You'll hear
a small heartbeat – hope – steady as a sonogram,

even though as yet, you can feel no movement.
Know that, within you, Paradise gestates.

III: [Gratitude]

Screaming Our Lungs Out

It follows that we are all sick, and that each of us would require a Sahara in order to scream our lungs out, or the shores of a wild and elegiac sea in order to mingle with its fierce lamentations our even fiercer ones.
      E.M. Cioran

Assume for a minute that we suckled
at similar teats, that the same five-fingered
hands match our bruises, that our thoughts
deepen homologous three-a.m. grooves.

We could swap clothes. Blindfolded
and given a spin, we would both stagger
in comedic misdirection, flinching
at the hilarity of unseen watchers.

We are exactly that part excised
from the other, that mercy, which
decades hence, we wish to recall,
to rescue like an infant from a dumpster.

Capacities

The orangutan, not even female, suckles
tiger cubs,

not in a bookplate of the Peaceable Kingdom
but in a zoo,

no jungle, no mate, for thousands of miles,
nothing but need

to be touched, clawed even, surrogate mother
to a tiger litter,

tilting a baby bottle between tiger whiskers,
lifting cubs

one by one to his shoulder, as if burping them.
He could teach

many a human father about presence, about
nuzzling close.

Who knows what we can love until it
pierces us?

Airborne

Hello, my ghost, my conjoined twin. Hello, beak and nictitating membrane. Hello, egg calcified in secret cloaca, yolk an albumen-swaddled flame. Hello, naked nestling, fledged to preen, barbs smoothed along vane. Hello, puff-pouched strut, bob, and mantle, the spread-winged seining of thermal and upgust. First, let us flare in a far-flung flock, then tuck heads beneath wings, together to roost, to brood, to regurgitate fine castings.

23.5°

the earth's mild obliquity that gives us seasons:
less and we'd lose our liquid water, more
and we'd swing yearly between extremes, boiling
and freezing by halves. Even our charmed axis
varies by degrees – ice ages – but always,
so far, we return to habitable. Will we always?
No telling. Wonder it happened at all.
How many planets whirl in the Goldilocks band
of distant stars, that sweet spot of liquid water?
Are we alone conscious and self-absorbed,
hashing everything in our grandiosity?
This planet is really on the verge of destruction
all the time, an astronomer marvels. All
the time! And we so petty, we tilted freaks of nature.

The Droughts Became More Frequent; the Wet Years Weren't Wet Enough

Lined at the pumps, we are thirsty,
a ghostly afterimage of progress,
clung to by children, strands of hair.

Air sounds a fugue through empty pipes,
voice after voice. Whole streets shift,
sinking into the tapped out.

Those we trusted squint pensively
at the dapple of swimming pools,
the rising walls of private reservoirs.

Our hands bloom through their fences,
but they are not garden people.
Eventually, we take up our bundles

and walk, bobbing like ants.
We move from carcass to carcass,
a whisper of dry stalks.

Gratitude

The grey parrot repeats *thank you*,
        not for having been wrested

from branches that ribbon
        from cloud-cover

where it would have wheeled
        in a bright flock,

but for the stuffed rabbit and the cake
        it received in a house

where it clings to a chair back.
        We also say thank you

for our narrow compass, all the way
        to the end of our chain

in a fenced yard. Thank you for
        this much dirt,

this water bowl, this fencepost, this job,
    this marriage, these kids.

Thank you for the stuffed rabbit,
    for the cake.

Where, then, should we go?

For decades we return to the same
small house on the cul-de-sac or
to the same apartment by the stairwell.
We know the trees that crook
outside our windows, their intimate signatures
of bark and knot hole. We share
a ready name for things, can lay our fingers
on the words we need. People look
where we point. We accomplish.
But something happens – a gradual
or quick rewiring. Suddenly, *That's my dog*
means *Hand me my sweater*. We lift
from the earth on unseen currents.
When young fists lose interest, we drift
away, are driven here and there
like packages. *Where should we go?*
our driver may humor us. *Right or left?*
Straight up, we answer, *into the dark.*

What We Are

(after Max Ernst 2 Young Nudes)

Your head a rasp, and mine also
as we lean into one another, blurring

already porous borders, making
a hash of geometry, but coupled

so nicely across what may be
a spathe or a blade, a spear or a lapel.

As children, we learn to point
to things and name them, but this

goes to hell in the end, in a mad
gesticulation for a glass of water

while barking, a groping after lost
things. You are sutured for no reason

I can discern, while I am pocked
and pitted. We blame our childhood

or the rough journey, but it may just be
the way we were made. A tracery

of brick, a careless daubing. Neither side
matches, but we have learned to celebrate

imbalance, not to care when eyes
peer in between our slipped slats.

Let them look. Even clouds
pause overhead for a glimpse.

Sad Night

We flee from our burdens across the causeways of night,
but the road has ghosted. We bring each other down,

then use the twisted limbs to keep above dark water.
If we survive till dawn, it is because we are guilty.

Ravens clack from purple-black hoods, eyes fierce
with knowing. We accustom ourselves to shame,

newlyweds twisting bright rings about captive fingers.
The story snags at the joint and cannot be sloughed.

Every two a.m., we relive the harrowing, always running
from a city that casts us out. We bruise beneath offal,

gag on the taste of iron. Grudgingly, dawn releases us
from where we sprawl in mud patterned by flailing.

The Slow Stipple

We have been married a great long while, the years extending filaments, gusting spores. Our photo albums flock mildew, ready for the yard-sale bin. Having fought and grappled much between bruised sheets, we weary of being pressed flat, anguish over our slow stipple. *Release us*, beg the crinkles at our eye corners, our turned-up lips. Perhaps some collagist will dissect us for scraps, not minding our brief visitation, hands resting on each other's shoulders, smiles held, even as mouths sever from cheeks, eyes from faces. There in the temple of scissors and glue, we will be offered up.

That Feeling

The falling man falls through the feed while, beneath him,
female soldiers serve in a bunker. Then, someone reposts,

and the order reverses, the women behind the blast door
now above the man who plummets. Both make the heart

hammer: the dead man, not yet dead, and the women, living,
but standing ready to dispense death. They are not the same,

yet they are juxtaposed. Coming upon them, our fingers
hover a moment; how much do we want to know, and what

will it cost us? For sixteen years, the falling man has triggered
panic: his knowing, his choosing, his leaping. We carry his death

like a burden we can never put down. We did nothing to stop it.
We think by not watching we are somehow absolved, but he falls

regardless. So too, the missiles. We will not launch them. Neither
can we stop them. Yet we are implicated in our Age, born into it;

its hectic pulse hammers within us. We shake. We tremble.
Our lines quiver across the page. No one wants to claim

the falling man. We refuse him, his helplessness, his nakedness
before our lenses, the wind pulling the clothes off his body,

our eyes doing the same. So too, the women, deep underground.
It was better before we knew they were there, each with her half

of the code, ready to key in the launch, ten missiles on standby.
Maybe their fingers will hover forever, poised for our generation

and for that of our children. We hope our hearts will quiet.
We have that guilty feeling as if we have done something wrong.

Dog-Walking in the Shadow of Pyongyang

We flip a coin over who walks
the dog, not tired, but edgy,
for the loser glances covertly
upward, listening for whistles,
siren-ready, side-eyeing each lot
for shelter. Somewhere in Pyongyang,
a finger hovers over a button, a head
cocks to catch the command
that will release the unmaker of worlds,
mine. The button-pusher is loyal,
me, reduced to caricature, and soon
to ash, all of us, web-stuck
in history. As with solar flares,
the big quake I'm told is coming,
or closer still, the millions arriving
next month to eclipse-gawk, my way
to cope is to deny, acting as if
and going about my business.
The Great Leader may render all

my insomniac panic moot –
aging, health-care, the planet,
my kids, my craft – a flame-out
to trace elements in an open crater.

Holdouts

Let them use voice recognition, embed hyperlinks,
turn and point their Oculus Rift, I will tappity-tap

the old-fashioned way, run my fingers over well-
worn keys, make your body and mine sing as they

have for decades. We don't need a mission to
No Man's Sky, our blue/grey is marvel enough,

and the known birds, the house finches, the
earnest robins and cheeky crows. Rediscovering

each other will get us no points, no upgrades
beyond making us ready to forgive our humanness

for a few more spins of this great rock through
charted space. I unlocked no chest to find

your skin, could find no buyer for it, worn as it is,
yet it delights me, hours of game-play left.

Dog-eared, laggy, prone to crash, we are so
yesterday, yet also, I hope, so tomorrow.

returning to petroglyphs

thumbs up to the smiley face and steaming shit-pile
    they are the words we cannot say,

cannot or will not, the Munch scream, the kiss-blower,
    punctuating the everyday, relieving

the black and white with winking irony, let's not
    be sticklers, late adopters, struggling

to light fires with bent twigs, nothing is as it seems,
    we are returning to petroglyphs, a language

universal – running bison, splayed hands that drip
    from cave walls, experience

pared down to the most essential – the wish for hap,
    a good hunt, the claim *I was here*

If You Don't Like What You See, Turn

We find ourselves amidst spattering. Sometimes droplets, sometimes skin, percussive, the heart both daub and paradiddle. Singular cells chorale blood's mad flood. All this to say we're never just *hell* or *halleluiah*. We summon spirits from air, shake them from shadows, decide battle's end with hands quick as scythe blades. How lucky never to be *just*. A flick of the wrist changes figure to ground.

The Breaths After and Between

Peace for our kind can only be walking towards
but never arriving. Somewhere between here and
there, something shatters it. We must kneel
and fashion constellations from shards.
Peace hazards buds, children playing in rubble.
Peace is the breath taken in the aftermath.
We continue living. We compose ourselves
into offerings for strangers to gather.
We remember surprise can also mean blessing.

New

There is no *she*, no *he*, just a cloisonné of lit
leaves, light, nature's newest greening of intention.
My *which?* reveals me antiquated, still bound
by the labeled figures in some old anatomy.
Cords and dials calibrate the soul's new
machinery, multiplex, an *us* within it.
There is refraction, a spangle of stars, water
droplets misting as on waxed fruit, small
hairs beading. The motes of your eyes float
before me. I want to swirl my hand across
the dappled air and clarify your nascent features
into something definite, to say *laurel, holly,
box, beech*, as if I held a field guide and could dog-ear
the page, making you easier to return to, each
splintered board no boundary, but a piece of home.

Acknowledgments

After the Singularity | *Sweet Tree Review*
Airborne | *Under a Warm Green Linden*
An Almost Imperceptible Percussiveness | *Alyss*
Bad Seed | *Tule Review*
By the Time they Opened You Up | *Poets Reading the News*
Capacities | *Peacock Journal*
Confession | *dis-articulations*
Demeter of the Ex-Urb | *Autumn Sky Daily*
Despite the Blaze | *Rise-Up Review*
Dog-Walking in the Shadow of Pyongyang | *The New Verse News*
East Egg | *Under a Warm Green Linden*
Eclogue | *Kestrel*
First Mover | *Psaltery & Lyre*
Futile | *Black Napkin Press*
Gaslighting | *2River*
Holdouts | *Rat's Ass Review*
If You Don't Like What You See, Turn | *Open: A Journal of Arts and Letters*
In This Poem, I Noun | *MiCRo*

Know | *What Rough Beast*
Land of Our Fathers | *Sierra Nevada Review*
Metta | *The Ekphrastic Review*
Make Portland Holy | *Kestrel*
Mission Baroque | *Dappled Things*
Nothing to Be Frightened of | *Poetry Circus*
Raisins Not Virgins | *What Rough Beast*
returning to petroglyphs | *Dream Fever*
Sad Night | *In Between Hangovers*
Sarracenia, the Siren Singer | *Free State Review*
Screaming Our Lungs Out | *One Jacar*
That Feeling | *Rattle*
The Breaths After and Between | *Lagan On-Line*
The Droughts Became More Frequent | *The Rise-Up Review*
The Slow Stipple | *3 Elements*
What There Is | *Malevolent Soap*
What We Are | *Open: A Journal of Arts and Letters*
Where, then, should we go | *Gone Lawn*

About the Author

When not teaching, Devon Balwit chases chickens in Portland, Oregon, USA. Her poems and reviews can be found in *The Worcester Review*, *The Cincinnati Review*, *Tampa Review*, *Barrow Street*, *Tar River Poetry*, *Sugar House Review*, *Rattle*, *Bellingham Review*, and *Grist* among others.

Nixes Mate published her book, *We are Procession, Seismograph* in 2017.

For more, visit **https://pelapdx.wixsite.com/devonbalwitpoet**

42° 19' 47.9" N 70° 56' 43.9" W

Nixes Mate is a navigational hazard in Boston Harbor used during the colonial period to gibbet and hang pirates and mutineers.

Nixes Mate Books features small-batch artisanal literature, created by writers who use all 26 letters of the alphabet and then some, honing their craft the time-honored way: one line at a time.

nixesmate.pub

www.ingramcontent.com/pod-product-compliance
Lightning Source LLC
Chambersburg PA
CBHW051808100526
44592CB00016B/2614